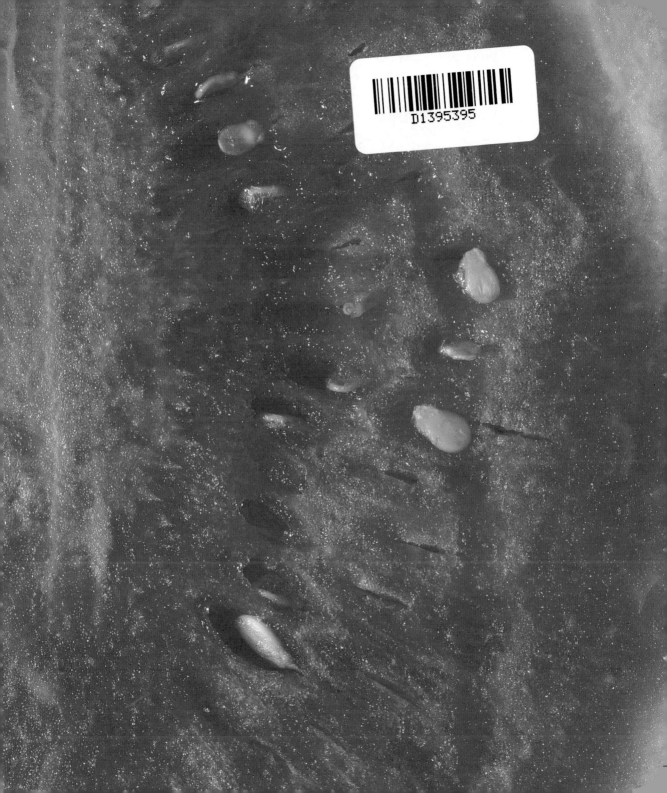

little book of drinks

innocent
little book of drinks

juices, smoothies & cocktails for work, rest & play

Credits

Recipes
Lucy Ede at innocent

Text
Dan Germain at innocent

Design
Adam Whitaker at Duffy

Watchful eye
Richard Reed at innocent

Editor
Louise Haines

Assistant editor
Mitzi Angel

Photography
Adam Whitaker
Tony Crolla

Additional photography
Clare Shilland
Ian Nolan

Illustration
Adam Whitaker

Home economist
Mandy Papadopolous

Recipe testers
Mrs Crabtree
Charlotte Bromley Davenport

First published in Great Britain in 2002 by Fourth Estate
A Division of HarperCollinsPublishers
77-85 Fulham Palace Road
London W6 8JB
www.4thestate.co.uk

A catalogue record for this book is available from the British Library.
Go and check if you don't believe us.

ISBN 1-84115-726-0

Design by Adam Whitaker at Duffy
Printed and bound in Hong Kong by Printing Express Limited.

Photography by
Adam Whitaker (pages 66-67, 68-69, 70-71, 72-73, 74-75, 76-77, 78-79,
80-81, 82-83, 84-85, 86-87, 90-91, 92-93, 94-95, 96-97, 98-99, 100-101,
102-103, 104-105, 106-107, 108-109); **Tony Crolla** (Cover and endpapers,
pages 16, 19, 20-21, 23, 46-47, 176); **Ian Nolan** (pages 132-133);
Clare Shilland (pages 13, 88-89).
All illustrations by **Adam Whitaker** at Duffy.

A big thank you

We've never written a book before but we've had a lot of fun doing it. The most important thing we've learnt is make sure you do it with some nice people who will help out a lot. That's why we're dead grateful to Cathy our agent for getting us the opportunity to write a book in the first place and to Louise, Mitzi, Iain, Kate, Nicole, Nicky and Michelle at 4th Estate for making sure that the book exists and is in the shops. Then there's Mr Whitaker at Duffy; illustrator, photographer and designer extraordinaire, who as well as lending us his photographs also lent us his brain in coming up with gags and ideas aplenty. And Hugh too, for getting involved when we were about to start getting told off by our publishers for being late. And not forgetting Uncle Flintham for his sound words of advice, Jason for his help with the cocktails and everyone at Duffy and Fruit Towers.

And finally, the biggest thanks goes to everyone who buys our drinks and this book. We promise to buy yours too.

Contents

A story with a happy ending

Hello. We're a little juice company called innocent and we make nice, fresh drinks that help people to be healthy. We set the company up three years ago, after we realized that our jobs were a bit boring and weren't very good for us either. In our old jobs, we worked late, ate rubbish food and topped it all off with a nice bit of TV when we got home. We were on first-name terms with the man at the dial-a-pizza place round the corner (ask for Rod if you're ever down there), not to mention the cast of E.R.

In 1998 we began talking properly about starting a company, something that we'd always thought about but never really got round to. Looking at ourselves and our friends, we thought of a million things that could improve our lives. Foil underpants and remote-controlled curtains – too futuristic. A bath that fills itself with water at exactly the right temperature – too dangerous (all that water and electricity). We even had a couple of dot.com ideas, but with hindsight, roastchicken.com probably wouldn't have caught on.

Smoothies seemed like quite a good idea, though. Take lots of nice fruit, put enough in a bottle to give you your daily fruit requirement and sell it in shops. People could do themselves some good, and it would taste nice too.

By 1999 we'd settled on that idea, but we needed to test out our theory. We bought £500-worth of fruit, turned it into smoothies and sold them from a stall at a little music festival in London. We put up a big sign saying 'Do you think we should give up our jobs to make these smoothies?' and put out a bin saying 'YES' and a bin saying 'NO', then asked people to put the empty bottle in the right bin. At the end of the weekend the 'YES' bin was full, so we went to work the next day and resigned.

Then we had to choose a name for the drinks. It took a long time but when we got to innocent it felt right. We call our drinks innocent because they are always completely pure, fresh and unadulterated. Naturally, the same principle applies to the drinks in this book.

Nowadays we still work late, but we enjoy what we do a lot more, and we're a lot healthier too. And innocent has grown – we've gone from having bedroom offices to working at Fruit Towers, and we make yoghurt thickies as well as our smoothies.

And we're all still friends, which is important.

Our little family of juice

Why we wrote a book

We decided to write a book when we started getting lots of calls on the banana phone from people asking us about how to juice at home and whether we had any suggestions for recipes. We love the idea of helping people to eat and drink as much fruit and veg as possible, therefore a book full of recipes and juicing tips seemed like a good idea. What's more, Lucy spends most of her days in our little juice kitchen here at Fruit Towers, making up lovely new healthy drinks, so we thought we should pass the nicest ideas on to you. We gathered our thoughts and spent lots of time playing around, making a mess and drinking lots of drinks. This book is the result.

We had two main criteria when choosing the recipes – the drink must taste good and do you good. That meant that everything in the drinks had to be natural and fresh. There's a whole spectrum of drinks in here – from ultra-healthy vegetable blends to our favourite chocolate shake. Of course, healthwise, you'd be better off drinking the fruit and veg drinks, but a little bit of what you fancy won't do you any harm, as long as you're sensible.

One thing that we haven't done in this book is add 'boosters' and nutritional supplements to the drinks. If you're using fresh, natural ingredients, the fruit and veg will give you all the nutrition you need. The bottom line is that nature provides. So our advice is to stay away from the grandiose promises of manufactured powders and pills and keep things nice and simple; a bit like us, really.

Using the book

Our recipes are divided into three sections: Work, Rest and Play. Fairly self-explanatory, isn't it? Of course, you are allowed to make Work recipes on Saturday mornings if you want to, but the general reasoning for splitting the recipes is as follows:

Work – Recipes at the healthier end of the spectrum. You'll find everything from instant breakfasts to nutrient-rich vegetable blends here, which will keep you active and full up all day. We want to stop you from nipping down the shop for some sweets and a can of pop, we really do.

Rest – It's a sunny Saturday afternoon and you want to make your loved one a more memorable drink than a cup of PG Tips. So this bit of the book is what you need – it's full of luxurious drinks made with strange and exotic ingredients. And chocolate too. So turn to the Rest section, breathe deeply and relax…

Play – Drink yourself healthy with the finest cocktail recipes we've ever seen, using tons of natural fresh ingredients. The alcohol might make you feel a bit giddy, but the fruit and veg will be making sure that you feel OK in the morning. You'll also find some recipes for the child in you.

All recipes will serve one greedy person or two caring, sharing people, unless described otherwise.

Ultimately, we hope that you will use the book in the spirit in which it was intended. The recipes are there to be messed about with; these are our favourites, but they're also jumping-off points from which you can create your own blends. We've included a few pages at the back of the book where you can note down your own secret potions. And you can email any good ones of your own to newrecipes@innocentdrinks.co.uk

That's about it. Before you get started, check out the other pre-recipe bumf. It's worth just finding out a bit about dealing with different types of fruit and veg, the equipment involved and the language that we use in the recipes before you get knee deep in pith, pips and peel. But first, a few words from our professor about the health benefits of juicing.

Juicing is good for you –
but don't just take our word for it

Hello. My name is Professor Millward. I am the Director of the Centre for Nutrition and Food Safety at the University of Surrey. In my daily work, I see the crucial importance of eating and drinking as many fruit and vegetables as possible.

Fruit and vegetables contain the vital nutrients needed to aid the body in its quest to give you a long life. They will help in the fight against heart disease, cancer, bone and skin disorders; they will give you natural energy when you need it and will keep your immune system alert and strong at all times.

Juicing is a great way to increase your intake of fruit and veg, allowing you to get hold of these vital nutrient packages. And juices make it easy for the body to absorb these essential elements. Interestingly, even the most complete supplement mix cannot begin to match the nutritional complexity of a fresh fruit and veg juice so, in my opinion, the juicer should be at the heart of everyone's kitchen, with juices taking pride of place at the dinner table.

If you're interested, there is a much more detailed section about what good work fruit and veg does for the human body. You'll find that in the back of the book.

In the meantime, get juicing. I've been working with innocent since they first started making juices and have always been impressed with their dedication to making the best and healthiest drinks. That work is continued in this book – so I hope you find time to enjoy some of their recipes.

Professor Joe Millward
Director of the Centre for Nutrition and Food Safety
University of Surrey

Looking after your fruit and veg

Keeping your juice cold

Most people find that fruit and veg juices are much more pleasant when served nice and cold, so why not keep your fruit in the fridge if you want your drinks cold? This also gives you the extra benefit of making your fruit last a bit longer. There are one or two fruits that don't particularly like being kept cold, such as bananas. But as a general rule of thumb, see which fruits are kept cold at the supermarket, and then do the same at home. Obviously, if you're trying to ripen a peach or plum, it won't get softer if you put it in the fridge. Leave these instead in a warm, dry place.

If you're out of fridge space, but you want a cold drink, you can always add ice. One exception to this is carrot juice. Adding ice to carrot juice doesn't really work as the juice is already quite thin, and melting ice just makes it thinner and less tasty. Warm carrot juice tastes insipid, so it is really worth making room for carrots in your fridge even if you can't find space for anything else.

These are general rules – some of our recipes use ice as an integral part of the drink, so we'll tell you when to use it. And some of the drinks are served warm – again, all instructions are contained in the recipes.

Freezing fruit and veg

Freezing fruit and veg is a good thing. The UK is not blessed with a particularly long fruit-growing season, nor can we grow a huge variety of different fruits in our climate. So it seems like a good idea to get hold of things when in season and save them for a rainy day in amongst your fish fingers and choc ices.

Freezing does not sterilize food; the extreme cold simply slows the growth of microorganisms, thus slowing down any changes that would normally spoil your produce. If you prepare, pack and freeze your fruit and veg properly, it will keep for at least 3 months, whereas if you leave apples and oranges at room temperature, they will go rotten after a couple of weeks.

Many people prefer to make drinks with frozen ingredients. The texture can be a bit thicker than it would be with fresh stuff, but any frozen fruit should be defrosted at least half an hour (if not longer) or you won't be able to taste the fruit for the ice.

Some advice for freezing your fruit and veg:

Prepare fruit as if you were about to juice immediately. This means peeling and cutting apples into wedges, or taking the stones out of cherries, nectarines, etc. Once you've prepared your fruit, stick it in some freezer bags or store in a freezer-proof plastic container. Don't use cling-film as it won't adequately protect your fruit. Whatever you use, try to make sure that it's airtight and waterproof, or your fruit will get ruined.

If you want to freeze vegetables, you should wash, trim and chop the veg as you normally would. Root veg should be blanched for a couple of minutes in boiling water before being chilled in ice-cold water for two or three minutes, patted dry, packed as per fruit and put into the freezer. Later on, you can defrost it and chuck it in the juicer.

Keep it clean
The one thing we can't stress enough is always wash your fruit and veg before you start to juice them. If you think about it, where do you think the man who picks strawberries all day out in the field goes to the toilet? I bet you anything he doesn't make it back to the farmhouse.

Juicing fruit and vegetables – the basics

The amount of fresh fruit and veg in your average supermarket is bewildering. And so is the array of equipment with which you can crush, juice and blend up all that nice produce. We used to find all of these gadgets a bit confusing, so here is the knowledge we've accrued in the last few years, to make things a bit simpler.

The three types of fruit and vegetables

For the purpose of making drinks, fruit and veg can be divided into three types – hard, soft and citrus. The general rule for what you do to each type of fruit and veg is:

Hard things (e.g. apples, carrots) should be juiced with a juicer

Soft things (e.g. strawberries, mangoes) should be blended with a blender

Citrus things (e.g. oranges) should be squeezed with a…wait for it…citrus squeezer

Hard

Soft

Citrus

When to juice, when to blend, when to squeeze

The following chart should make things easier, too. It shows you which technique you should employ on each type of fruit and veg used in this book, in order to get the most out of your produce.

Fruit/veg	Juice	Blend	Squeeze
Apple	•		
Apricot	•	•	
Avocado		•	
Banana		•	
Beetroot	•		
Blackberry		•	
Blackcurrant		•	
Blueberry		•	
Carrot	•	•	
Celery	•	•	
Cherry		•	
Cranberry		•	
Cucumber	•		
Date		•	
Fennel	•		
Fig		•	
Grapefruit		segments	•
Grape		•	
Guava		•	
Kiwi		•	
Lemon		•	•
Lime		•	•
Lychee		•	
Mango		•	
Mangosteen		•	
Melon, Cantaloupe	•	•	
Melon, Galia	•	•	
Nectarine	•	•	
Orange		segments	•
Passion fruit		•	
Paw paw		•	
Peach		•	
Pear	•	•	
Pineapple	•	•	
Plum	•	•	
Rambutan		•	
Raspberry		•	
Redcurrant		•	
Spinach	•		
Strawberry		•	
Watermelon	•	•	

NB You'll notice that there are a few fruits that we recommend that you can juice **and** blend. For example, if you juice a pineapple, you get a very sweet liquid, but you don't get a lot. If you blend one, you'll get the pulpy bits too, so you end up with a thicker purée.

The equipment involved

There are three essential bits of kit for home-juicing – juicers, blenders and squeezers. This section details what they are, what they do and what to look out for when buying them. We've also included the equipment that we have used, and while we're not saying it's necessarily the best on the market, it has certainly done us proud.

Juicers

A juicer is something that extracts juice from hard fruit and veg, e.g. apples, carrots, beetroot, pears. There are three main types of juicer:

Centrifugal – The easiest to get hold of, and the cheapest. Whole fruit and veg, skin and all, are fed into a fast spinning grater (don't worry, it's kept well away from your fingers). Juice is forced through the small holes in the grater, whilst the pulp, seeds and other bits stay in the grater, or are sent to a waste container. Juice is usually collected in a jug or cup that should be supplied with the machine.

Masticating – You get a bit more juice from these juicers (hence they are a little more pricey). They chew and grind up the fruit and veg before forcing the mush through wire mesh with great force.

Hydraulic – The most efficient (and most expensive) juicers. They exert large amounts of pressure on your fruit and veg after it has all been chopped and crushed with revolving cutters. You are left with lots of dry pulp and high-grade juice.

Buying guide

Juicers can be a pain to clean. The following features could save you a lot of time and effort:

- Dishwasher-friendly components (if you have a dishwasher).

- Removable waste containers. Many centrifugal juicers expel waste from the grater area to a removable container. If yours doesn't, you'll have to empty the grater more often.

- Disposable filter papers can be manna from heaven if you juice often. They'll save you from cleaning the grater or mesh of your juicer. But they can be a bit fiddly.

Some people believe that centrifugal juicers aren't that great – they generate lots of heat, which may harm enzymes contained in the juice, and they may also add quite a bit of oxygen into the mix, which can react to destroy certain vitamins if not drunk quickly.

However, we think that is taking everything a bit too seriously. Buying a juicer is a positive step. Whatever juicer you buy, you'll be adding health to your diet and joy to your kitchen. And you can start out with a centrifugal one for under £50, then upgrade to the masticating/hydraulic types, which cost £200+ if you really get into it.

What we use
A Moulinex 753 juicer – quite compact for a centrifugal juicer. The fruit and veg are fed into the machine via a hole on the top, and you have to push them down into the grater area with the poker (as it is not technically known). All of the waste is fed into a separate unit that can be easily removed and emptied, and the juice comes out of a spout at the front. It doesn't have a huge capacity, but has been bashed about by us and still does what it's supposed to do. Having said all of this, it is a relatively old model, and you might find it difficult to get hold of. The newer Kenwood JE550 does all of the same thing, and a bit more. It costs about £30.

Juicing tips
Unless washed thoroughly, your juicer can retain flavours from previous juicing sessions. Putting something with a strong yet neutral flavour through it (e.g. an apple or a peeled lime) should shift any unwelcome flavours.

**Centrifugal juicer –
the one we use**

Blenders

Blenders, a.k.a. liquidisers, usually take the form of a jug that sits on a base that houses the spinning motor. They are suitable for mashing up soft fruit and veg, as well as blending juices with other ingredients. You'll need to remove inedible bits (pips, peel, stalks) before blending.

Buying guide
When buying a blender, look for the following:

- Speed settings – the more the better. You can use the low ones for the initial chopping, moving to higher settings to thoroughly blend the drink. Some blenders have a pulse setting that is great for a quick blitz.

- Blenders look very similar, so check how much power they have (it's usually written on the underside of the base). More power equals less hassle, and 350 watts is as low as you want to go; 500 watts is ideal.

- A glass jug is much easier to clean and won't break as easily as some of the flimsier plastic ones (unless you drop it, of course).

- Get a blender that has a jug that plonks straight into the base. You'll become annoyed with the type that requires safecracker-style twists to make it secure.

- If you have a dishwasher, you'd be mad not to choose a blender with dishwasherable parts.

**Our blender –
nice and sturdy**

**For the juice chef
with limited space**

What we use

A Russell Hobbs 3901 blender – a nice-looking black and chrome machine, very suitable for the aesthetes amongst you. It's got 3 speeds and a pulse setting, and has a glass jug that feels nice and sturdy and will go in the dishwasher. It's heavy enough so that it doesn't feel like it'll fly off the base unit, even when whirring away at high speeds. It also crushes ice, and all of the bits come apart to make it easy to clean. Costs about £50.

For those with more limited space in the kitchen, there's always the option of a hand-blender. Braun's 500-watt Multiquick is more powerful than many conventional blenders, and it's dishwasher-proof too. What's more, it comes with a lovely ice-crushing attachment. Costs from £35.

Blending tips

Sometimes your mixture will stick to the sides of your jug. If this happens, turn your blender off at the mains and give the jug a few downward jerks to get the mixture back down onto the blades. If it's just too gloopy, add a bit more liquid to get it to the required consistency.

Start blending with liquids and soft fruits, ending with harder fruits. The hard stuff will blend more easily with lubrication.

Citrus presses

These range from the timeless glass number which everyone has seen at their granny's house, to funny ones that work like one-armed bandits, to electric ones. Our thoughts are to keep it simple and don't spend loads of money – the old basic models work just fine and help you get out all of the juice that you need.

Just like your granny's, but a bit more posh

Oranges don't stand a chance

21

Cocktail equipment

We used a blender and a juicer to come up with all of the fresh juices used in our cocktails, but then they have to be incorporated into the boozy mixture. So here are some other things that you might need.

Shaker

The classic bit of cocktail equipment, the traditional metal shaker. Put your ingredients in, jam on the lid, then shake. Pretty easy, really.

Strainer

A disc of wire mesh through which you pour your mixture. It stops you from getting all the big bits of fruit, veg and excess ice into your glass, i.e. it prevents all the fibrous pieces of ginger from messing up your Lemon Grass and Ginger Martini. Use a small sieve if you don't have a strainer.

Bar spoon

A long spoon with a twisted stem. It will come in very useful for stirring, mixing, crushing and squashing. But its most fancy function is for pouring champagne. As we all know, champagne fizzes up when it is poured straight from the bottle. Place the bar spoon in the glass and pour the champagne slowly so it runs down the stem of the spoon. The liquid will helter-skelter down the stem and your friends will gasp in astonishment.

Work

9:00AM

Spinach and spice

This recipe will make two generous shots of the most revitalising juice possible. It will sort you out after a hard night out on the tiles, so you can bolt it down quickly and then hide under your desk for the rest of the morning.

ingredients

2 or 3 big handfuls of fresh spinach
2 large apples (Royal Gala if you can get them)
1/2 a lemon
Fresh grated nutmeg

what to do

Remove the stalks from the spinach and put the leaves through the juicer.
Pour the juice into a jug.
Cut the apples into wedges, juice and add the juice to the jug.
Add the freshly squeezed lemon juice and nutmeg.
Stir and serve over ice.

Use your spice rack if you haven't got fresh nutmeg to grate.

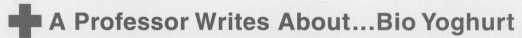# A Professor Writes About...Bio Yoghurt

Bio is short for probiotic, a term which comes from the Greek for 'in favour of life'. The probiotic cultures found in bio yoghurt do two main things – firstly, they help restore your intestinal microflora balance, and secondly, they inhibit the growth of 'bad' bacteria. The beneficial flora that normally flourish in the intestinal tract can be destroyed by factors such as stress, processed food, pesticides, chlorinated drinking water and high-fat, high-protein diets. If you consume or are susceptible to any of these factors, adding bio yoghurt to your diet will maintain the balance that your digestive system needs. Bio yoghurt also promotes the good health of the large intestine and keep us better equipped to fight the growth of disease-causing bacteria. Examples of good bacteria are Bifidobacterium bifidus and Lactobacillus acidophilus.

PROFESSOR JOE MILLWARD

Strawberry and banana lumpie

The original breakfast in a cup – fruit, yoghurt and fibre. You'll be very full, very happy and you might even be able to squeeze past 11 a.m. without wanting to eat your sandwiches.

ingredients

5 strawberries
1 medium banana
4 tablespoons of bio yoghurt
A couple of mouthfuls of milk
1 teaspoon of clear honey
1 tablespoon of rolled oats
1 tablespoon of wheat flakes
1 tablespoon of raisins, or you could use muesli as a substitute for these last three.

what to do

De-stalk the strawberries.
Place the banana, strawberries, yoghurt, milk and honey into the blender and whizz until smooth.
Add the oats, wheat flakes and raisins (or muesli) to the blender.
Whizz to desired consistency.

This will serve one large glass as a breakfast drink or two glasses if served as a snack. Watch out for muesli with added sugar. You shouldn't really need it – honey and raisins are naturally sweet enough.

I'm on the mobile...what?...the mobile...yes...yes...yes...no... grapefruit yes, well, always get nice heavy ones, like a baby's head, yes baby's head h-e-a-d, shocking I know, couldn't believe they had the cheek to be out together, well pink ones are best, very sweet, lots of beta-carotene apparently, which is really good for the skin, well I can't believe they changed it to Olay quite frankly, so, can you hear me? Yes, oranges, well Valencia are very juicy and sweet, great for juicing, well the Parma ham was too salty so I'd go for the chicken, anyway, you could always use Navels, the ones with the pokey out belly button, but Navel juice will go a bit funny after a couple of days apparently, I know he had it removed but the waiting list was hideous, or you can use Jaffa, they're the ones with the pale skin, absolutely, got the shock of my life when I walked past him just now, practising a speech, listen I've got to go, you're breaking up...

Pink grapefruit, orange & lime

What do you want for breakfast? A soggy Danish? Nice cold slice of last night's pizza? Or vitamins B, C, folic acid, beta-carotene and potassium in a glass? If it's the latter, consult the recipe below.

ingredients
2 oranges
1 pink grapefruit
1 lime

what to do
Cut the peel from one of the oranges.
Remove all the pips and place in the blender.
Squeeze the juice from the grapefruit, lime and remaining orange into the blender and whizz.

How To Get Away With Not Doing Anything
#01 Carrying Files

A great method of work avoidance. Just
pick up a few files and have a wander
round the office, maybe stopping to chat
to people, but stopping the chat at your
discretion with an ominous 'I've got to get
on – I've got these files to sort out.' More
fool the person who asks you what's in your
files. You will, of course, have constructed
an elaborate story centred around the last
five years' sales figures, and nobody will
stick around to hear that one.

Lemon juice, cayenne & maple syrup

This potion is a tried and tested favourite of those who are detoxing. It sounds a bit scary, but tastes surprisingly good and is great for the morning after, or when feeling generally run down. Maple syrup provides energy, lemon juice adds sharpness and vitamin C, and the cayenne pepper helps to open small blood vessels, which allows the body to get rid of stored toxins. If you're still hungover, you can always slack off (see opposite).

ingredients
2 lemons
1/4 teaspoon of cayenne pepper
1 or 2 dessertspoons of maple syrup (or honey)
Hot water from the kettle

what to do
Squeeze the lemons. Put the juice into a bowl and add the cayenne pepper and maple syrup. Give it all a stir. Add an equal quantity of hot water to the lemon mixture and mix them together. Now drink from your favourite supping mug and feel the vapours soothe your headache/hangover/ general malaise.

✚ A Professor Writes About...Bits In Your Juice

A key ingredient in this recipe is the orange. Vitamin C is the thing we rightly know and love oranges for, but the flesh also contains bioflavonoids, which enable vitamin C to work more effectively and be absorbed into your cells more efficiently. Vitamin C and bioflavonoids will build up your antioxidant defence system, so don't be afraid of bits in your juice.

PROFESSOR JOE MILLWARD

Nectarines, oranges & dates

Good morning. In case you hadn't noticed, humans are naturally slow at the beginning of the day. What you need is a good dose of fruit sugars to restore your brain's natural sugar levels, which are at their lowest at dawn. Dates happen to be an amazing source of natural sugars, which is why we invented this drink.

ingredients
1 large nectarine
2 oranges
2 dates (Medjool are the best)
2 tablespoons of bio yoghurt

what to do
Halve the nectarine and remove the stone.
Cut into wedges and place in the blender.
Squeeze the two oranges and pour the juice into the blender.
Remove the stones from the dates and place in the blender.
Add the yoghurt and whizz until smooth.

Tired and irritable? Then use 150ml of freshly squeezed orange juice instead of squeezing your own.

BANANA WORKSHOP

- Bananas are great – they're rich in fibre and they're a funny shape too

- During an exhausting day at the office, your body loses important vitamins like B6 and C as well as minerals like potassium

FIG 1

- Bananas replace these nutrients and help you maintain peak performance. Now you know why great sportsmen and women and Pete Sampras chomp bananas

- When making smoothies, use bananas that are ripe and speckled brown – they'll be lovely and sweet

Classic strawberry & banana smoothie

This is a slight variation on the very first recipe that we put in a bottle and sold. It's not difficult, it's not clever, but it's nice and thick, it tastes lovely and it will give you lots of healthy energy. So here it is.

ingredients
6 strawberries
1 banana
1 tablespoon of bio yoghurt
1 orange

what to do
De-stalk the strawberries and stick them in the blender, along with the banana and bio yoghurt. Squeeze the orange, add the juice to the blender and whizz everything until smooth.

Melon, kiwi & white grapes

If you're looking for a quick pick-me-up before that important Rotary Club meeting, then have a swift measure of this fruit blend. The natural fruit sugars and vitamin C will have you peaking at the right time, and Sir Ronald will be impressed as you outline plans for a new children's playground down at the primary school.

ingredients
1/2 a Galia melon
2 or 3 handfuls of seedless white grapes (does anyone know how they grow seedless grapes?)
2 small kiwi fruit

what to do
Remove and discard the rind and the seeds of the melon.
Place the melon flesh and the grapes in the blender and whizz.
Cut the kiwi fruit in half and scoop out the flesh.
Add this to the melon and the grapes and give it a quick whizz.

Take care not to over-blend the kiwi fruit as the seeds can break up and give you a little dry tickle at the back of your throat. Ahem. And did you know that one kiwi fruit contains as much vitamin C as two oranges?

✚ A Professor Writes About...Grapefruit

Sharp as a knife but a lot more edible, grapefruits are one of nature's finest all-rounders. They contain all the right things to ensure you have a healthy heart, especially vitamin C. Their antioxidants keep cells healthy and, touch wood, cancer free. Pink grapefruits also give you a good shot of anthocyanins, which are thought to be another important component in the fight against cancer.

PROFESSOR JOE MILLWARD

Carrot and pink grapefruit

Another veritable powerhouse of nutrients, antioxidants and valuable minerals, this fine breakfast juice has more waking-up power than eight really big gongs being gonged right next to your bed.

ingredients
5 carrots
2 pink grapefruits

what to do
Top and tail the carrots.
Put the carrots through the juicer.
Pour the juice into a jug.
Squeeze the grapefruits and pour the juice into the jug.
Mix and drink.

Still in bed? Then avoid squeezing two grapefruits by making sure you've got 200ml of bottled stuff in your fridge.

Apples and pears

This recipe contains lots of vitamin C, lots of pectin and lots of nice English fruit, providing you with all the energy you need to roll out the barrel.

ingredients
2 large apples (try to use Russet for their smoky flavour)
2 large pears
1/2 a lemon

what to do
Cut the apples and pears into wedges.
Put them through the juicer and pour the juice into a jug.
Squeeze the juice from the lemon and add to the jug.
Give it a good stir and serve.

Too busy doing the Lambeth Walk? Then use 100ml bottled, freshly pressed apple juice instead of juicing your own.

How To Get Away With Not Doing Anything
#02 Rehearsing a Speech

Head for the nearest empty office or
meeting room. Once inside, start to pace
up and down, pretending to read from
a piece of paper. It should be apparent
to passers-by that you are practising
a speech, a fact that can be accentuated
by scratching your head and occasionally
taking your eyes off the paper to look at
the ceiling, in the classic 'memorizing
position'. Anyone looking in on you will
think 'Ooh that looks a bit heavy' and
will leave you in peace.

Peach and redcurrant

Packed full of potassium, vitamin C and beta-carotene, this lovely, thick drink should take your mind off that mountain of paperwork. If not, follow the advice given opposite.

ingredients

1 apple (Royal Gala if possible)
1 large, juicy peach
1 orange
2 or 3 handfuls of redcurrants

what to do

Cut the apple into wedges, put them through the juicer and pour the juice into the blender.
Halve the peach and remove the stone.
Place the halves in the blender.
Squeeze the orange into the blender.
Add the redcurrants and whizz everything until smooth.

Redcurrants have a fairly short summer season. You could use raspberries instead if they are in your local shop. Or you can use frozen redcurrants.

From left: Nectarines, oranges & dates; Melon, kiwi & white grapes; Carrots and oranges; Banana and cinnamon thickie; Carrot, beetroot & celery; Peach, strawberries, melon & mango; Spinach and spice

➕ A Professor Writes About...Carrots

Carrots are rich in carotenoids, amazing nutrients that help the body combat conditions such as asthma, heart disease, arthritis and cancer, and will help to maintain healthy skin and immunity. Interestingly, drinking carrot juice allows you to absorb carotenoids more easily than if you were eating carrots, which makes staying healthy even more simple. And your Mum was right – you'll be able to see in the dark if you consume lots of carrots. You will actually have assimilated lots of beta-carotene, which aids sight once the body has converted it to vitamin A.

PROFESSOR JOE MILLWARD

Carrot juice

There's nothing better than carrot juice. If you find the idea of vegetable juice a bit odd, then here is your starting point – sweet, thirst-quenching and horrifyingly good for you. We know you might think it's a bit funny, but please be a brave soldier for Mummy.

ingredients
5 large carrots

what to do
Wash the carrots and remove the tops and tails.
Cut carrots in half and put them though the juicer.
Drink straight away.

Keep your carrots in the fridge if you want nice, cold juice. Warm carrot juice tastes insipid and adding ice makes an already thin juice much too watery. You can save on the washing-up by freezing batches of carrot juice. Drink the juice on the day of defrosting.

Carrot, kiwi, orange & pineapple

Here's a fine detox juice for you. Each ingredient is a rich source of antioxidants and will help sort out your aching head and conscience after a heavy night, giving you all day to impress people at work.

ingredients

2 large carrots
1/4 of a medium pineapple
1 orange
1 kiwi

what to do

Top and tail the carrots.
Put them through the juicer and then pour the juice into the blender.
Remove the skin from the pineapple and slice the flesh into the blender.
Squeeze the orange and add the juice to the pineapple and carrot juice.
Whizz until everything's blended together.
Cut the kiwi in half and scoop out the flesh into the blender.
Give everything one quick final whizz.

Just managed to get out for five minutes, told them I needed a natural break, exactly, gasping for a fag, carrots, yes well they're absolutely full of carotenoids, no not fags, carrots, and the beta-carotene and lutein in them will keep your skin healthy and boost your immune system, well it's much cheaper in World of Leather but you wouldn't catch me dead in there, yeah and amazing for the eyes too, well I wouldn't mind seeing him in the dark I can tell you, really good for heart disease as well, erm it must have been three weeks now, yes what? carrots, top and tail them, gets rid of the impurities, ooh and did you see that thing in Marie Claire about the horse? turns out the best English carrots are around between June and September, lovely deep orange colour just like those Clinique girls, oops, hang on a minute I think they want me back in there...

Carrot and orange

The two powerhouses of the juice world unite to prove that together they are stronger.
You should feel this one working its antioxidant and vitamin-enriched magic in seconds.

ingredients
4 large carrots
2 oranges (get hold of Valencia if possible)

what to do
Remove the tops and tails from the carrots.
Put the carrots through the juicer and pour into a jug.
Squeeze the oranges, pour the juice into the jug and stir until fully blended.

You can add fresh grated ginger or fresh chopped mint for a bit of a kick. And use shop-bought freshly squeezed orange juice if you don't want to squeeze your own, although that would be horribly lazy as there are only two ingredients to begin with.

✚ A Professor Writes About...Apple & Ginger

Apple and ginger are a great combination. To make sure you get the most out of apples, don't peel them before juicing, as they contain a lot of their nutrients in the skin. You should always give them a good wash, though. Apples are a great source of pectin, which helps keep cholesterol low. And they contain vitamins A and C, as well as providing a good amount of dietary fibre. Ginger has been used as a cure-all for centuries. The ailments that it is said to soothe include motion sickness, nausea and indigestion. What's more, it may help to relieve a sore throat. Just remove the skin and chew on a small piece.

PROFESSOR JOE MILLWARD

Carrot, apple & ginger

The nation's favourite carrot blend. If you don't feel healthy after drinking this, ring 1-800-VIRTUOUS and ask for your money back.

ingredients

3 large carrots
2 small apples
1 thumbnail of fresh ginger

what to do

Top and tail the carrots and put them through the juicer.
Pour the juice into a jug.
Cut the apples into wedges and put them through the juicer.
Add the juice to the jug, too.
Peel the ginger and finely grate into the carrot and apple juice.
Stir and serve.

UNDERSTANDING BEETROOT

- Always use raw beets – scrub the skin & put them in the juicer

- Feeling brave? You can always stick beetroot tops in your juicer too, as they are full of iron

- Vacuum-packed beets aren't very juicy and taste vinegary

- If you can't find fresh beetroot, use other hard root veg such as parsnips or carrots

- Beetroot juice turns your wee pink

SO NOW YOU KNOW

Carrot, beetroot & celery

Problem: you are weak. You eat bad food and drink too much. Sometimes you stay up late and listen to the disco music. Your work is suffering and you smell a bit too. You need answers. Solution: be strong, drink this life-giving stuff and feel much better.

ingredients
3 large carrots
1 small beetroot
2 celery sticks
1/2 a lemon

what to do
Top and tail the carrots and beetroot and cut into chunks.
Put them through the juicer, then pour the juice into a jug.
Trim the celery and put it through the juicer too.
Mix the celery juice with the carrot and beetroot juices.
Squeeze the lemon and then add the juice to the jug.
Serve over ice.

Peach, strawberries, melon & mango

A curious worker is a happy worker. Always asking questions, always learning and occasionally breaking stuff. A curious worker would be very interested to find out that what you eat dictates how you smell. People in South-east Asia say that Europeans smell of milk, because of the amount of dairy produce we stick down our necks. Ergo, if you drink lots of beer and eat a fried breakfast every day, Ralph Lauren won't be naming a fragrance after you. So drink this fresh, fragrant fruit juice and save money on eau de cologne.

ingredients
5 strawberries
1 peach
1/4 of a melon (Cantaloupe is best here)
1/2 a mango

what to do
De-stalk the strawberries and put them in the blender.
Halve the peach and remove the stone.
Place the flesh in the blender along with the strawberries.
Remove and discard the rind and seeds of the melon.
Cut the flesh into chunks and add to the blender.
Peel the mango, slice the flesh into the blender and whizz.

✚ A Professor Writes About...Bio Yoghurt Again

Bio yoghurt is good for people who are lactose intolerant, which means they find it difficult to digest milk or, more specifically, to digest the sugar in milk (lactose). These people lack a digestive enzyme called lactase that breaks down lactose, leaving them liable to suffer from stomach pains and diarrhoea, which can occur up to twelve hours after consuming excess lactose. Fortunately, the fermentation of milk into yoghurt converts most of the lactose into lactic acid (the substance responsible for yoghurt's sharp taste). What's more, the live cultures in bio yoghurt help to break down the rest of the lactose, allowing those who are lactose intolerant to enjoy the benefits of a dairy product without feeling ill.

PROFESSOR JOE MILLWARD

Banana and cinnamon thickie

The perfect drink for the modern executive. Cinnamon has blood-pressure-lowering effects and bananas give a long, slow burn of energy, getting you through your high-powered day of buying, selling and making those funny shapes with paper clips.

ingredients
1 apple (Royal Gala if possible)
2 bananas
4 tablespoons of bio yoghurt
1 teaspoon of honey
1/2 teaspoon of freshly ground cinnamon

what to do
Cut the apple into wedges and put them through the juicer.
Pour the juice into the blender with the other ingredients.
Whizz until smooth.

Sneak 50ml of bottled, freshly pressed apple juice into the drink if you can't be bothered to press the apples yourself.

How To Get Away With Not Doing Anything
#03 Standing by the Photocopier

Nobody ever wants to get involved in
this activity, so make the photocopying
room your personal domain (deckchair
optional). One sheet of A4 can last you
for hours, and by using the same sheet
over and over, you'll be doing your bit
for the environment. For extra style
points, the timeless 'lid-up' approach
will add minutes of stalled time, as
you start to dismantle the machine,
looking for a fictitious paper jam.

Apple, banana, pineapple & lemon

There isn't much this juice won't do. A rich source of nutrients, it will also help digestion, regulate acidity in the stomach and enhance your immunity. You should be able to find these ingredients year round, so there are no excuses for not making this wonderful smoothie, unless you can't be bothered.

ingredients
1 apple (preferably Russet)
1 lemon
1 banana
1/4 pineapple
1 person to make this drink for you

what to do
Cut the apple into wedges and put them through the juicer.
Pour the juice into the blender.
Squeeze the lemon and pour the juice into the blender, adding the banana too.
Remove the skin from the pineapple and slice the flesh into the blender.
Whizz everything until smooth.
Serve over ice or add four or five ice cubes to the blender.

50 ml of bottled, freshly pressed apple juice will do if your juicer is on strike.

Beetroot, pear, apple & ginger

Working late is one of the hazards of office life, like accidentally stapling your fingers together or getting off with Janice/Roger at the Christmas party. When working late, give yourself a chance by drinking this drink – it's packed full of energy-providing nutrients, meaning you'll still be going strong at 11.30 p.m.

ingredients
1 small, cute, raw beetroot
1 apple
1 pear
A squeeze of lemon
1/2 a thumb of ginger

what to do
Top and tail the beetroot and cut it into chunks.
Put them through the juicer and pour the juice into the blender.
Cut the apple and pear into wedges.
Put them through the juicer and add them to the beetroot juice.
Add the squeeze of lemon.
Peel and finely grate the ginger into the blender, then whizz and serve over ice.

Rest

Rambutan, paw paw & lime

Rambutans are eaten as a chaser with durian, a large, spiny fruit especially popular in South-east Asia. We didn't fancy using durian in this drink as it has a very distinctive aroma, a bit like ripe cheese on a hot summer's day. So we've used something a lot more palatable from the same region – the paw paw. Take a sip, lie back and think of Thailand.

ingredients
1 apple
1 lime
1 small paw paw
8 rambutans (or lychees)

what to do
Chop the apple into wedges, put through the juicer, and add the juice to the blender.
Squeeze the lime and pour the juice into the blender.
Peel and de-seed the paw paw and scoop the flesh into the blender.
Peel and stone the rambutans and place the flesh into the blender.
Whizz until smooth.

Our favourite beach activity – searching for cigarette ends. Sometimes you can even find ones that are still a bit dry.

Jamaican carrot punch

You might want to drink this one lying down.

ingredients
2 large carrots
150ml milk
4 tablespoons of condensed milk
1 teaspoon of freshly grated nutmeg
Seeds of half a vanilla pod

what to do
Scrub, wash, top and tail the carrots before grating them into a bowl.
Add the normal milk to the carrots and leave to soak for an hour whilst reading chapters
two and three of 'War and Peace'.
Filter out the grated carrot pieces (they don't go in the drink; where they do go is up to you)
and pour the carrot-soaked milk into the blender.
Add the remaining ingredients and whizz.

To remove the seeds from the vanilla pod, cut the pod lengthways then scrape the little seeds out.

Passion fruit, honey & coconut

A great one for sitting on the dock of the bay. We recommend informing the neighbours if you're going to whistle.

ingredients
1 passion fruit
1 banana
2 tablespoons of coconut cream
1 teaspoon of honey
1 orange
3 tablespoons of bio yoghurt

what to do
Cut the passion fruit in half and scoop out the flesh into the blender.
Add the banana, coconut cream and honey and give it a little whizz.
Squeeze the orange and add the juice to the blender.
Add the yoghurt and give it one last whizz.

Take care not to over-blend the yoghurt, as it can lose its consistency and become thin.

Don't drop your camera.

74

Paw paw, pineapple, lime & ginger

If everything goes to plan, this drink should remind you of a rare yet memorable sunny beach holiday. If not, there's always Center Parcs.

ingredients

1/4 of a pineapple
1 paw paw
1 lime
1 orange
A thumbnail of fresh ginger

what to do

Remove the skin from the pineapple and slice the flesh into the blender.
Cut the paw paw in half and discard the black seeds and white pith.
Scoop out the flesh into the blender.
Squeeze the juice of the lime and orange into the blender.
Finally, peel and finely grate the ginger into the blender and whizz.

Passion fruit and guava

All of the different fruits in this drink came from a long way away just to be with you.*
Separated from their families, they made the long journey to your local shop, so give
them a fitting send-off and make them into this thick, delicious and relaxing drink.

ingredients

passion fruit
large guava (or 2 small ones) – make sure they are really ripe and soft
banana
1/2 a lime
2 apples

what to do

Cut the passion fruit and guava in half and scoop out the flesh into the blender.
Add the banana and the juice of the lime.
Cut the apples into wedges and put them through the juicer, adding the juice to the blender.
Whizz.

Guava pips are edible, but it's really important to use ripe fruit. If you don't, the pips will be
really hard and the fruit won't have much flavour.

Apart from the apples.

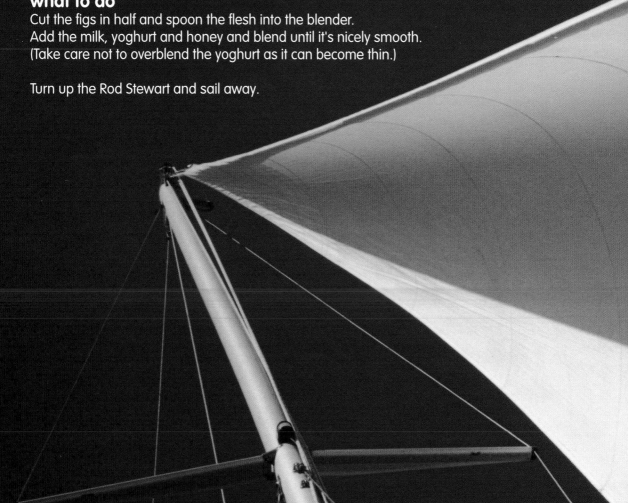

Yoghurt, honey & figs

Pure Greek luxury. And we're not talking about two weeks full board in Corfu.

ingredients
4 fresh figs
100ml milk
6 tablespoons of Greek bio yoghurt
2 teaspoons of runny honey

what to do
Cut the figs in half and spoon the flesh into the blender.
Add the milk, yoghurt and honey and blend until it's nicely smooth.
(Take care not to overblend the yoghurt as it can become thin.)

Turn up the Rod Stewart and sail away.

Pineapple, mango & lime

Lie back, breathe deeply, drink this drink and you'll find that things look a little different.*

ingredients
1/2 a small pineapple
1 small mango
1 orange
1 lime

what to do
Remove the skin from the pineapple and slice the flesh into the blender.
Peel the mango and slice the flesh into the blender with the pineapple.
Squeeze the orange and the lime, add the juice to the blender and whizz.

You could use 75ml of bottled, freshly squeezed orange juice instead of squeezing your own oranges.

*But don't get too involved in all that 'how big is the universe' stuff. You'll only scare yourself.

Watermelon, strawberries & lime

Oh, for the memories of summer. The sound of wasps buzzing, ice-cream vans tinkling and water pistols sprinkling. Call up that summery feeling any time by listening to the sound of crunchy watermelon in your mouth.

ingredients
6 strawberries
1/4 of a watermelon
1/2 lime
1 small church*

what to do
De-stalk the strawberries and chuck them into the blender.
Remove and discard the rind and seeds of the watermelon.
Throw the flesh into the blender along with the strawberries.
Squeeze the juice from the lime into the blender and whizz.
Serve over lots of ice.

* not really

Cucumber, mint & kiwi

So genteel, so elegant, so green. This is one to drink late on a summer afternoon, while playing croquet on a manicured lawn or surveying the grounds of your country estate. Obviously, that doesn't stop you from drinking it while fixing your bike in the garage, but there's a time and a place for everything.

ingredients
1/2 a cucumber
1 large apple
A few fresh mint leaves
2 kiwis

what to do
Cut the cucumber into chunks and the apple into wedges.
Put them both through the juicer and pour the juices into the blender.
Roughly chop the mint leaves, place into the blender and whizz.
Cut the kiwis in half and scoop the flesh into the blender.
Whizz one last time and serve immediately, over ice cubes.

Just don't care? Use 50ml of fresh pressed apple juice from the shops if you don't want to DIY.

Blackberries, plums & apples

As you're driving down the country lanes of this great land, sit back in your seat, feel full of pride* and wave at the fruit trees, just like the Queen.

ingredients
4 red plums
2 handfuls of blackberries
2 large apples (Russet work best here)

what to do
Place the blackberries into the blender.
Halve the plums and remove the stones.
Cut them into quarters and add to the blackberries.
Cut the apples into wedges, put them through the juicer, then add to the plums and blackberries.
Give everything a good whizz.

Blackberries are only around for a short season during autumn, but you can usually find them in the freezer cabinet of your local supermarket. In desperate times, you can substitute raspberries, blackcurrants or redcurrants instead of blackberries.

*Hands up if you know the words to the second verse of 'God Save the Queen'.

From left: Mango and cardamom thickie; Strawberries and black pepper; Paw paw, lime & ginger; Yoghurt, honey & figs; Blackberries, plums & apples; Fresh mocha

Crème fraîche and lychee

Nice sunny day. Nothing to do except sit in a stripy deckchair. The only thing missing is a person who will make this rich, creamy drink for you. So give us a ring and we'll see if Adam and Daisy can come round and help.

ingredients
8 lychees
2 oranges
3 tablespoons of crème fraîche (ooh, fancy)

what to do
Peel and stone the lychees. Put the flesh into the blender.
Squeeze the oranges and add the juice to the blender.
Finally add the crème fraîche (ooh la la) and whizz.

Don't over-blend as the crème fraîche will get too thin.
Preparing lychees can be a bit messy. Peel and stone them over a bowl to catch that juice.

Don't fall asleep in the sun, Grandad. Remember what happened last time.

Non-boozy milk

Almost as relaxing as boozy milk, but for drivers.

ingredients
250ml milk
2 cardamom pods
2 cloves
1 teaspoon of brown sugar
Freshly ground cinnamon to taste

what to do
Put all of the ingredients into a saucepan.
Whisk lightly over a low heat until warm.
Remove the cardamom pods and cloves, unless you like chewing on them.
Pour into your second-favourite mug.
Sprinkle with cinnamon.

Want to make the drink during the ad break? Then pour all of the ingredients into
a microwave-proof jug, whisk and microwave for one to one-and-a-half minutes.

Strawberries and black pepper

Summer with a bite. This drink will refresh and perk you up, thanks to the addition of a little black pepper. And it sounds posh too.

ingredients
1/4 of a watermelon
10 strawberries
Black pepper to taste

what to do
Discard the rind and seeds from the watermelon.
Cut the flesh into chunks and place in the blender.
De-stalk the strawberries and add them to the watermelon in the blender.
Add black pepper and whizz.

Strawberries, watermelon & mint

Cool, ice-textured and breath-fresheningly delicious.

ingredients
6 strawberries
A handful of fresh mint leaves*
1/2 a watermelon

what to do
De-stalk the strawberries and put them in the blender.
Add the mint leaves to the blender and whizz.
Remove and discard the rind and seeds of the watermelon and cut into chunks.
Add the watermelon flesh to the blender and whizz until smooth.
Pour into an ice-filled glass.

Watermelon takes a while to blend down. It's much easier when the strawberries are put into the blender first.

*If you can't find fresh mint, toothpaste, Polos and chewing gum will not do.

Avocado, chilli & ginger

Fortune favours the brave. This drink sounds more like a dip, but have faith. It's very good.
It's something that a friend told us about, and he discovered it in Dharmsala, home of the Dalai Lama.
Which might mean that enlightenment is only a couple of sips away.

ingredients
1 large apple (Russet would be good)
1 small, fresh green chilli (or more – the heat is up to you)
A thumbnail of fresh ginger
150ml milk
3 tablespoons of bio yoghurt
1 medium avocado, nice and ripe and stoned
1 lime
5 or 6 ice cubes

what to do
Cut the apple into wedges and put them through the juicer.
Pour the juice into the blender.
De-seed and finely chop the chilli – don't rub your eyes.
Peel and finely grate the ginger, then chuck it and the chilli into the blender.
Add the milk and yoghurt and whizz once, then spoon the avocado flesh into the blender.
Squeeze the lime into the blender, whizz it once more and serve over ice.

White chocolate smoothie

This drink is very thick and very rich, a bit like some pop stars. It could be likened to drinking a white fluffy cloud.

Ingredients
6 (yes, 6 is enough) chunks of white chocolate
1 teaspoon runny honey
A small bunch of white grapes
1 banana
1 sharp apple (Granny Smith or Cox would be nice)

what to do
Melt the chocolate in a bowl set over a pan of simmering water.
Pour the melted chocolate into the blender with the honey, grapes and banana.
Cut the apples into wedges and put them through the juicer, add the juice to the blender and whizz it up.
Cool it in the fridge before drinking or serve in an ice-cold glass.

Because the chocolate gets hot when melted, it's really important to chill the glass, otherwise the drink gets slightly warm.

This recipe was kindly sent to us by Nadine Akle, innocent drinker and recipe thinker.

Mangosteen, melon, coconut & lime

As rare as nice sunsets in Lincolnshire, you may find it hard to get hold of mangosteens. So if you ever see any, snap them up. They have an amazing perfume, quite unlike any other fruit. Combined with the other ingredients in this recipe, you get a beautiful thick drink that could be the best in this book. But then that's just one person's opinion.

ingredients
6 mangosteens
1/4 of a watermelon
1/2 a lime
1 dessertspoon of coconut milk

what to do
Prepare the mangosteens by breaking the shell to reveal the white fleshy segments.
Put these into the blender.
Remove and discard the rind and seeds of the watermelon and cut into chunks.
Squeeze the lime into the blender along with the watermelon flesh and coconut milk and whizz.

You can substitute lychees for mangosteens. Use ten lychees instead of six mangosteens.

This is a picture of a nice sunset in Lincolnshire

Mango and cardamom thickie

India. Mysterious and magical land, full of many strange and wonderful things, including sitars, cows and lovely lassi drinks. This is our own fragrant, sweet and filling take on the lassi. Nirvana is at the bottom of your glass.

ingredients
2 large apples
1 medium-sized mango (Alphonso are our favourite)
3 tablespoons of bio yoghurt
1 teaspoon of clear runny honey
1 cardamom pod

what to do
Cut the apples into wedges, getting rid of the bits you don't normally eat.
Then put them through the juicer and pour the juice into the blender.
Peel the mango and slice into the blender.
Add the yoghurt and honey too.
Crush the cardamom pod with the back of a spoon and remove the seeds.
Discard the pod, crush the seeds in the same way and add them to the blender.
Whizz all the ingredients until smooth.

Can't be bothered to juice apples? You can use 100ml of bottled, freshly pressed apple juice if you're feeling lazy.

Fresh mocha

An indulgent coffee drink for the people who like coffee, chocolate and sunsets.

ingredients
8 pieces of chocolate (not optional)
250ml milk
1 cup of espresso
5 or 6 ice cubes (optional)

what to do
Melt the chocolate in a bowl set over a pan of simmering water.
Place all the ingredients in the blender together and whizz.
Serve over crushed ice, or add the ice cubes to the blender and whizz once more.

You can also melt chocolate in the microwave by breaking the chocolate into chunks and placing them in a bowl. Microwave for one to one-and-a-half minutes. If you don't have an espresso maker, substitute with one or two teaspoons of instant coffee dissolved in an espresso-ish amount of hot water.

Boozy milk

Long winter nights are a bit of a pain. But you can positively embrace them by making a nice, warming mug of boozy milk when you get in from work. A couple of sips and you'll soon be contentedly curled up on your couch.

ingredients

250ml milk
2 capfuls of dark rum
1 teaspoon of runny honey
Freshly ground cinnamon to taste
1 settee

what to do

Put all of the ingredients into a saucepan.
Whisk over a low heat until warm.
Pour into your favourite mug.
Sprinkle with cinnamon.

Feeling lazy? Don't want a dirty pan? Then pour all of the ingredients into a microwave-friendly jug, whisk and microwave for one to one-and-a-half minutes. For ground cinnamon, get some cinnamon sticks and grind them into dust using a pestle and mortar. Or cheat and consult your spice rack.

Play

Here's M.
M is saying hello.
Hello, M.
Shall we all say hello to M?

Really real custard

ingredients
1 egg yolk
150ml milk
1 teaspoon of caster sugar
Seeds from 1/2 a vanilla pod

what to do
Beat the egg with a little of the milk.
Place the remaining milk, sugar and vanilla seeds
in a saucepan, heat until lightly simmering.
Pour the warm milk mixture into the beaten egg in a
bowl and stir well. Rinse the pan and return mixture
to the pan and stir until it thickens. You will need four
tablespoons of custard for the rhubarb and custard
recipe – that means a little left over for the cook.

Rhubarb and custard

Although more often found in Grandma's kitchen, rhubarb and custard also make a fine drink. The sharp taste of rhubarb is nursed by the apple, and the custard makes it into a great thing for pudding fans across the world.

ingredients
2 large apples (Russet would be best)
3 large sticks of rhubarb
4 tablespoons of custard
1 small piece of chopped stem ginger

what to do
Put wedges of apple through the juicer.
Cut the rhubarb into chunks and place in a saucepan with the apple juice.
Cover and stew over a gentle heat for five or six minutes until the rhubarb is soft.
Leave it to cool.
When the rhubarb and apple are cool, pour them into the blender.
Add the custard and ginger and blend until smooth.

You can use any kind of custard to make this recipe. We made our own from scratch (see opposite) but you can use the powdered kind (made with milk). There are also tinned/fresh versions. It all depends on personal taste and how much time you have on your hands.

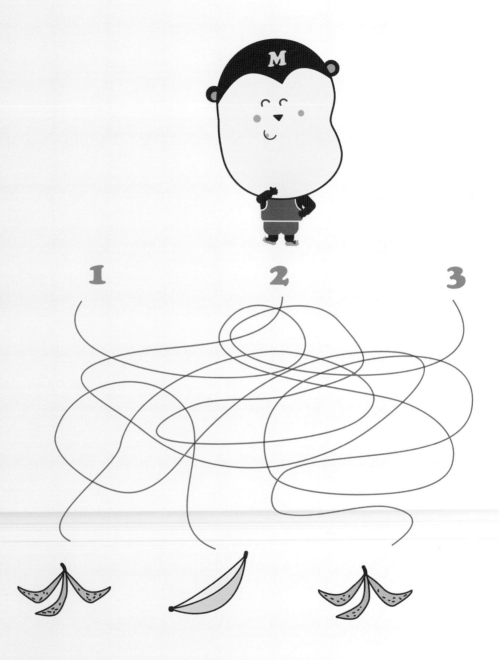

Can you help our friend M find the nice tasty banana without slipping up on the smelly brown banana skins?

Peanut butter and banana lumpie

This recipe is filled with bananas, peanuts and the taste of childhood, allowing you to happily regress to more gentle days filled with kiss-chase and marbles.

ingredients
1 medium banana
3 tablespoons of bio yoghurt
125ml milk
1 tablespoon of crunchy peanut butter

what to do
Put all ingredients into the blender and whizz.
Drink.

Now go and do some finger painting or potato prints.

Excuses for eating chocolate

• Quality chocolate (when it has a high concentration of cocoa)
is as an excellent source of minerals such as iron, calcium
and potassium, as well as vitamins A, B1, C, D and E

• The cocoa bean is the richest source of magnesium in nature.
Magnesium deficiency is linked with heart disease,
hypertension and diabetes

• And women get an extra reason to eat chocolate as pre-menstrual
syndrome has also been linked with a lack of magnesium
(which results in a progesterone dip, causing the associated mood swings).
Again, make sure the chocolate is high in cocoa solids, not sugar

• It's raining again

Real chocolate milkshake

No description required really. It's not like you're not going to make it, is it?

ingredients
8 pieces of milk chocolate
250ml milk
A scoop of vanilla ice-cream
5 or 6 ice cubes

what to do
Melt the chocolate in a bowl set over a pan of simmering water.
Mix the melted chocolate with two tablespoons of the milk and stir until thoroughly mixed.
Put the remaining milk and the chocolate mixture into the blender.
Add the ice-cream and five or six ice cubes and whizz.

Late for the dentist's? Then cheat your way to melted chocolate – break it into chunks and place in a bowl. Microwave for one to one-and-a-half minutes.

If you prefer a less sickly chocolate taste, use a continental chocolate with a higher cocoa percentage.

Got a sweet tooth? (Yes.) Like a little texture in your shake? (Of course.) Then throw in half a Crunchie bar at the end and blend. If you're more malty, try adding two digestive biscuits, then blend.

Fennel is an anti-spasmodic, which helps to relieve intestinal cramps and stomach pain. You can make a tea from fennel seeds as a way to maximise absorption and cure your ills.

Fennel has many different uses in the world of alternative medicine. It is said to increase the flow of breast milk and improve sex drive (though not necessarily in that order).

Fennel has the aroma of aniseed, just like Pernod. And if you've ever had a bit too much Pernod then you'll be familiar with the smell.

Florence fennel is the variety most often seen in the supermarket, and is characterised by its bulbous bottom and wispy green fronds at the top.

Funnel sounds a bit like fennel but even M knows you find them on top of ships, not next to the broccoli.

Fennel and blackcurrant

A non-alcoholic Pernod and black drink, as made by nature, rather than Stacey and Derek down at The Golden Fleece.

ingredients

1 head of fennel – about the size of your hand
1 apple
1/2 a lemon
A handful of blackcurrants (fresh or frozen)

what to do

Trim any leaves from the top of the fennel and cut into chunks.
Put them through the juicer and then pour the juice into the blender.
Cut the apple into wedges, put them through the juicer and add to the fennel juice.
Squeeze the juice from the lemon into the blender.
Add the blackcurrants and whizz.

Posh Word Search

Bufty Simpkins and Hugo Ponsenby-Smythe will have M booted out of the polo club before you can say 'time for tiffin' if you can't help him find eleven posh things in the grid below.

```
T  H  T  O  P  H  A  T  O
B  U  D  O  N  I  S  A  C
E  N  E  C  A  S  J  Y  I
T  T  Y  A  C  H  T  G  E
O  I  A  V  I  S  R  F  C
C  N  Y  I  C  O  L  M  A
S  G  K  A  C  D  L  F  L
A  L  O  R  U  F  E  O  A
Q  D  U  H  G  M  W  S  P
```

gucci

top hat

caviar

yacht

corgi

palace

hunting

ascot

casino

polo

ok ya

Peach Bellini

Ooh look at you on your yacht moored just off Amalfi with your D&G wraparounds. That drink looks posh too.

ingredients
1/2 a ripe peach
1/2 a bottle of champagne (or prosecco for a 'real' Italian Bellini)

what to do
Halve the peach and remove the stone.
Muddle the flesh in a mug.
Strain the muddled peach flesh through a sieve, then divide into two champagne glasses.
Slowly top up each glass with champagne.

Muddling is a flash cocktail term for crushing the fruit with the end of a rolling pin.

Champagne fizzes up when it gets poured straight from the bottle into a glass. To stop this from happening, put a bar spoon in the glass and pour the champagne slowly so it runs down the stem of the spoon. The wine will twist down the stem like a small child on a helter skelter, and your drink won't fizz up as much.

To intensify the flavour, you could add a dash of peach brandy, and to remain truly authentic, use prosecco (Italian sparkling wine) instead of champagne. Prosecco is produced in the northern province of Treviso, just south of the Alps.

Love's young dream

The most romantic cocktail in the book, it features Mr Raspberry and Miss Blackberry sharing a bottle of champagne together. This lovable and bubbly drink is definitely the one to serve while whispering sweet nothings to your special friend.

ingredients
4 raspberries
2 blackberries
1/2 a bottle of champagne

what to do
Take two champagne glasses and place two raspberries and a blackberry in each glass.
Crush them with the flat end of a bar spoon (a teaspoon will do).
Slowly top up with champagne.

Taste the fruit first to make sure it's sweet. Tart fruit will make a mess of that expensive champagne.
If the fruit isn't sweet, you could add a teaspoon of crème de mûre (blackberry liqueur) to each glass.

Pears

• Pears are a good source of pectin, which provides soluble fibre and reduces blood cholesterol levels

• Pears are low in substances that cause food allergies

• Greengrocers get really fed up with people walking past their stalls and shouting 'nice pear'

• Pears are related to apples, and there are nearly as many different varieties; over 3000 when somebody last counted

• Pears also contain a nutrient called boron, which increases mental alertness and helps prevent osteoporosis

William the Uncorkerer

It's pear time. And that's a good time as far as we're concerned. This little drink consists of nothing but pears and champagne, and as a result is insanely simple and uniquely delicious.

ingredients
1 big juicy pear (as the name suggests, we recommend William's pears)
1/2 a bottle of champagne

what to do
Cut the pears into wedges and juice them.
Fill four champagne glasses a third full with pear juice.
Slowly top up with champagne.

Other types of pear will do, but make sure they are big and juicy.
If you have any Poire Williams Eau de Vie (first choice) or Poire Williams Liqueur, you should add a generous dash to the pear juice before topping up with champagne.

Golden rules for making the quintessential martini

Use really good quality spirits. Because martinis are so simple, more than any other cocktail they rely on having good quality ingredients.

Martinis should be served ice cold to take the edge off the spirit, but should never be watered down. Add ice to the cocktail shaker last, shake quickly and pour out straight away. Pour through a strainer so you don't get ice and bits in your drink.

To keep the drink cold it is worth serving martinis in chilled glasses. Stick them in the freezer half an hour before you get busy in the kitchen.

Refrain from making jokes that you're like a martini because you're available 'anytime anyplace anywhere'.

Cucumber martini

You don't even know what sophistication is until you've tried this drink. The delicate elegance of the cucumber, the strong guiding hand of the gin, the parfum of the herbs. It's all so precious, so beautiful. I fear I must have a lie down.

ingredients
1/4 a cucumber
100ml gin
3 x 2cm segments of coriander stalk
2 or 4 mint leaves
A handful of ice
2 teaspoons of sirop de gomme (optional)

what to do
Juice the cucumber – leave a little skin on for texture, but not all of it, as it will make the drink bitter.
Pour the juice into the shaker, along with the gin, coriander stalk, mint leaves and ice.
Shake and strain into chilled martini glasses.
If you find it too bitter, add sirop de gomme for sweetness.

Sirop de gomme is a cocktail essential, so it's worth hunting down a bottle. If you don't have any, you can make some by reducing equal volumes of caster sugar and water in a pan over a low heat. You should end up with a thick sugary paste; your very own sirop de gomme.

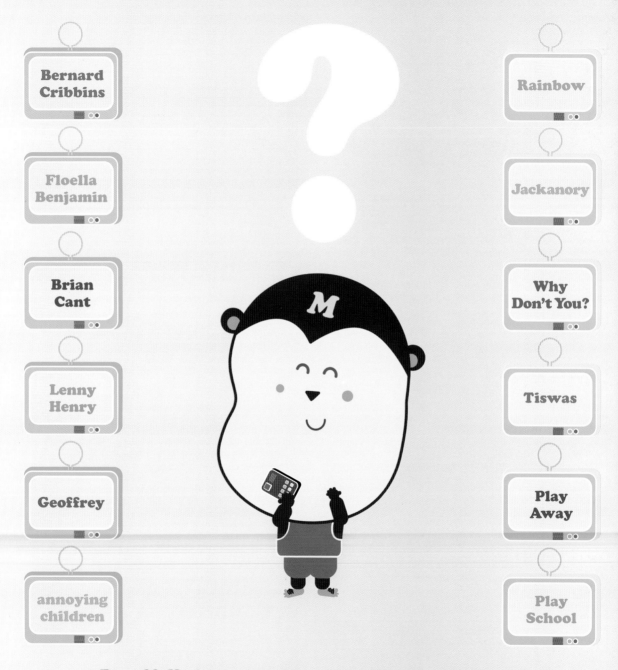

Bernard Cribbins

Floella Benjamin

Brian Cant

Lenny Henry

Geoffrey

annoying children

Rainbow

Jackanory

Why Don't You?

Tiswas

Play Away

Play School

Poor M. He loves watching kids' TV shows from the
70s and early 80s, but he's got all confused.
Can you help him match the presenters to the show?

The Stu Francis martini

For a while, the world was Stu's oyster. He was the main man on Crackerjack – he could do no wrong. We don't know what he's up to now, but wherever he is, he remains in our hearts. So let's all crush a grape or two and dedicate this drink to him.

ingredients
A thumbnail of ginger
3 seedless black grapes
3 seedless white grapes
100ml of vodka
A handful of ice

what to do
Peel the ginger and put it into the shaker along with the grapes.
Squash and crush the ginger and grapes in the bottom of the shaker.
Add the vodka and some ice to the shaker and shake hard.
Strain into two chilled martini glasses.

Things About Ginger

• It's a great cure for nausea – simply chew
on a small piece

• It can prevent embarrassment at dinner parties as
it helps reduce pesky indigestion and intestinal gas

• It's a good source of zingiberene and
gingerols, which stimulate circulation

• It's a great name for a cat

Lemon grass and ginger martini

Get one over on Joyce and Neil from the golf club by serving this at your next drinks evening. Their pineapple-and-cheese-on-a-stick hedgehog will soon be forgotten as people gawp in wonder at this very fine drink. And like all martinis, it delivers a real kick.

ingredients
1/2 a thumb of lemon grass
1 thumbnail of ginger
150ml vodka
A handful of ice

what to do
Remove and discard the tough outer leaves from the lemon grass and peel the skin from the ginger.
Place the ginger and lemon grass in the cocktail shaker and crush them up.
Add the vodka and ice.
Now shake.
Now shake a bit more.
And a bit more.
Fun, isn't it?
Rub the rim of two chilled martini glasses with a fragrant piece of lemon grass. (Don't use the outer layers as they won't give off any zest.)
Strain the drink into the chilled glasses.
Garnish each drink with a sliver of lemon grass.

Left to right:Detox/retox; Love's young dream; Cucumber martini;
Fennel and blackcurrant; Innocent Mary; Hibiscus iced tea

133

M's Magic Banana Trick

Amaze and impress your friends with M's ingenious banana trick.

Take a pin and carefully push it into the banana, wiggling it back and forth so that you slice the banana inside without making any obvious marks on the skin. Repeat this so that you are creating a stack of coin-shaped slices inside the banana.

Dress up as a magician if that's your sort of thing.

Get a friend to peel the banana.

If you've done it properly then 'abracadabra', the banana will already be sliced and will fall apart in your friend's hands.

Banana Caipirinha

Cachaca is a kind of rum popular in South America, made by distilling the liquids extracted from sugar cane. Its name means 'burning water'. Ouch.

ingredients
1 banana
1/2 lime
4 teaspoons of demerara sugar
Lots of crushed ice
1 bottle of cachaca (meaning you'll have plenty to spare for another round of drinks)

what to do
This drink is made in its own glass.
Use tumblers with a good heavy base if you've got them.
Muddle half a banana in each tumbler.
Chop the half of lime into four equal pieces, and squeeze the juice from two pieces into each tumbler.
Drop two squeezed lime pieces into each tumbler and add two healthy teaspoonfuls of demerara sugar to each glass.
Mush the banana, lime and sugar up with the end of a rolling pin.
Top up the tumblers with crushed ice, then fill them with cachaca.
Give everything a good stir.

To make crushed ice, wrap some ice cubes in a clean tea towel and get to work with your rolling pin.

This recipe will work with any fruit that you fancy – bananas, berries, nectarines, peaches. Traditional caipirinhas are made without additional fruit – just lime, sugar, ice and cachaca.

High as a kite

Like scissors, this drink is very sharp. It's also quite strong. As a result, we recommend you do not operate heavy machinery or attempt any c-r-a-z-y stunts while drinking it.

ingredients
1 pink grapefruit
100ml of gin
20ml of Campari or Aperol
A handful of ice cubes
2 slices of pink grapefruit to garnish

what to do
Squeeze the grapefruit and pour the juice into the cocktail shaker.
Add the gin, Campari and ice to the grapefruit.
Shake and then pour into two empty tumblers.
Garnish with a slice of pink grapefruit.

How to open a coconut

First, you need to remove the milk so you don't create a mess. To do this, puncture the largest of the three 'eyes' you will find on the top of the shell, using a screwdriver or similar. Drain the milk into a glass.

Every coconut has a natural fracture point in its shell. To find it, place the coconut on a flat surface, and hit it with the back of a knife blade about a third of the way from the smaller end of the shell. Rotate the shell slightly and hit the coconut again. Repeat this several times.

You will see a fracture develop. Now insert the tip of the knife in such a way that you can easily get at the white 'meat'.

Coconut love

The sweet, sweet coconut. Something that one can indeed fall in love with. This special drink gives you everything that is good about the coconut and a little bit more.

ingredients
1/2 lime
4 small guavas
100ml golden rum (you can use clear rum, but the golden stuff tastes nicer).
2 teaspoons of coconut cream
A handful of ice cubes
Fresh coconut to garnish

what to do
Squeeze two quarters of lime into the cocktail shaker, then drop in the bits of lime.
Cut the guavas in half and scoop out the flesh into the blender.
Whizz into a purée and add to the lime in the cocktail shaker.
Add the rum, coconut cream and some ice to the shaker.
Shake very hard.
Strain the mixture into two empty tumblers and grate some fresh coconut on top as a garnish.

If you can't find fresh guavas, you can always use tinned guavas, which you can find in oriental and West Indian food shops. Drain the syrup and give the guavas a good rinse before using in the recipe. Tinned guavas are usually pink in colour, as opposed to the green-white of fresh guavas.

Whisky and orange twist

This cocktail kicks against the old-fashioned way of serving whisky. It's a slightly weird mixture, but it definitely works. Trust us, you'll be on the dancefloor in no time.

ingredients
4 ripe apricots
100ml Chivas Regal whisky
A shot of Stone's ginger wine
A splash of apricot brandy (optional)
Lots of ice
Ginger ale
Orange twists to garnish

what to do
Halve the apricots and remove the stones.
Place in a blender and whizz.
Put the apricot purée in a shaker with the whisky, ginger wine and apricot brandy.
Add ice and shake.
Strain and pour into two ice-filled tall glasses.
Top up with ginger ale and garnish with a twist of orange.

Use nectarines or peaches if you can't find apricots. Remember that they are bigger than apricots, so use one peach/nectarine for every two apricots.

The Life of Noel

Noel was born in Hampshire in 1947.

Noel's TV CV includes Multi-coloured Swap Shop, The Late Late Breakfast Show (amusingly scheduled on a Saturday tea-time) and the inimitable Noel's House Party. Oh, and Telly Addicts.

Noel loves being approached in the street by people who ask if he can swap a Lego Moonbase for an Atari.

Noel Edmonds

A multi-coloured cocktail of truly mythical proportions. Loads of fruit, loads of booze and a rather nice garnish. We wouldn't swap it for anything.

ingredients
4 guavas
1 passion fruit
1 mango
2 bananas
100ml golden rum
Lots of ice
1/2 a passion fruit to garnish

what to do
Cut the guavas and passion fruit in half and scoop out the flesh into the blender.
Peel the mango and bananas and slice the flesh into the blender. Add the rum and whizz.
Strain the mixture into two ice-filled glasses.
Garnish each with a quarter of passion fruit.

If you are left with some of the mixture in your strainer/sieve, force it through with the back of a spoon.

Hibiscus iced tea

I bet your Gran would like this one. And if you want to see if she's all right to drive afterwards ask her to knit in a straight line.

ingredients

1/2 a thumb of fresh ginger
100ml golden rum
1 lime
4 cloves
100 ml cold hibiscus tea (use earl grey if you can't get hibiscus)
A flake of fresh cinnamon
Lots of ice
Soda water

what to do

Peel the ginger and muddle with the rum in a cocktail shaker.
Squeeze the lime into the cocktail shaker and add the cloves, tea and cinnamon.
Add some ice and shake.
Strain into two tall ice-filled glasses and top up with soda water.

Make hibiscus tea with dried hibiscus flowers, available from good health-food stores. Don't use hibiscus flowers from your garden because they will taste horrible and make your stomach a bit funny. Hibiscus makes your wee pink.

Free Radicals

- Free radicals are unstable oxygen molecules found in the human body. They are unstable as they only contain a single electron and are therefore keen to find a partner

- Free radicals are the baddies that cause the damaging process of oxidisation in the body (the same process that turns an apple brown once you've bitten into it)

- In the quest to find a partner, they attack and damage healthy cells and transform DNA – the process that can lead to the development of cancers

- Fortunately, the human body can counter the effect of free radicals with antioxidants, but to do so the body needs a constant supply of these good guys

- Fresh fruit and vegetables are the best source of antioxidants, which explains why we always go on about the need to eat lots of nature's finest

Detox/retox

We say drink yourself healthy. The antioxidants in the fruit will combat the damaging effects of the free radicals found in booze, and the natural source of vitamins will assist your body in detoxing. Looks like you're plain out of excuses for not drinking this drink.

ingredients
1/4 of a pineapple
1 mango
2 apples (Cox's work well here)
3 large strawberries
100ml vodka
Lots of ice
A good handful of blueberries

what to do
Remove the skin from the pineapple and mango and slice the flesh into the blender.
Chop the apples and feed the slices through the juicer. Pour the juice into the blender.
De-stalk the strawberries then put them into the blender with the vodka and whizz.
Pour into tall ice-filled glasses.
Garnish with blueberries.

How to get fit with a watermelon

Ripe watermelons can weigh up to 8kg.
They are essentially nature's medicine ball.
If you're feeling active and there's a watermelon
and partner around, try the following exercises.

1) Lie down on the floor opposite your partner
with the soles of your feet touching. Then take
it in turns to do a sit-up holding the watermelon,
then throwing it to your partner. Repeat 40 times.

2) Build up your pecs and upper arms by holding
the watermelon to your chest with both hands and
throwing the melon outwards to your partner who
catches it and does the same back. Repeat 40 times.

3) If you're feeling brave, you can test and enhance
your stomach muscles by lying on the floor and
getting your partner to drop the watermelon on
your stomach. Clench your stomach muscles to
avoid being winded.

4) Take your watermelon for a walk.

Watermelon chez vous

We've always fancied coming round to your house, so make a lot of this and put it in a big jug with some bits of lemon. We'll pop in after work.

ingredients

1/8 fresh watermelon
100ml lemon vodka
50ml triple sec (buy some in France if you go on holiday there)
Lots of ice
1 lemon
1 can of ginger beer

what to do

Remove and discard the rind and seeds from the watermelon.
Place the flesh in a blender and whizz.
Put the watermelon purée into a cocktail shaker along with the vodka, triple sec and a few ice cubes.
Squeeze the lemon, add the juice to the cocktail shaker and shake.
Strain into two tall glasses filled with ice.
Top up with ginger beer.

If you haven't got any lemon vodka, use normal vodka with an extra squeeze of lime/lemon.
Get a little watermelon if you can – it will be sweeter and they have fewer pips. A really small one will have no pips at all.

1) without vodka

2) with vodka

Innocent Mary

Just like a Virgin Mary but without Mr Branson's official endorsement – this is the definitive recipe for the classic brunch drink. Adding vodka is slightly less innocent, but we won't tell if you don't.

ingredients
3 cherries
1/2 a lemon
1 tin of tomatoes
100ml lemon vodka (optional)
A few bits of chopped coriander stalk
Some chopped chives
A good splash of Worcestershire sauce
Tabasco to taste
A dash of dry sherry
A couple of pinches of celery salt
Salt and pepper
Lots of ice

what to do
De-stone the cherries and put them in the blender.
Squeeze the lemon and add the juice to the cherries (keep the squeezed lemon bits for decorating the glasses).
Add the tin of tomatoes, vodka, coriander, chives, Worcestershire sauce, Tabasco, sherry, celery salt and seasoning to the cherries and lemon.
Then blend.
Prepare a couple of tall glasses which you have rimmed with a salt and celery salt mixture (moisten the rims of the glasses with a bit of lemon and then plonk the glasses on to a plate which contains a thin sprinkling of salt and celery salt).
Fill glasses with ice and pour the liquid in.

All About Prunes

- Prunes are dried plums

- Although not known for it, prunes are a
  great source of iron and potassium

- Prunes do have a slight laxative effect.
  This assists the bowel function, and enhances the
  elimination of toxins

- The best prunes in the world are believed to come from
  Agen, a small town in France where they have been
  grown for over 800 years

- The inhabitants of Agen have heard all the jokes before

Prune express

There's nothing better than an alcoholic drink that is good for you. Apart from maybe a nice hot bath and an early night. That aside, this drink is packed full of fruit, with added Grand Marnier to get you up and at 'em.

ingredients
2 apples
1 large pear
100 ml prune purée
100 ml Grand Marnier
Lots of ice
Soda water

what to do
Put the apples and pear through the juicer and pour the juice into a shaker.
Add the prune purée and Grand Marnier to the shaker. Add ice and shake.
Pour into two ice-filled glasses, then top up with soda water.

Prunes come in many different forms. We use tinned prunes in water, rather than the ones in syrup. Just drain them, remove the stones and then blend – each tin should make about 100ml of prune purée. If you've only got dried prunes, they can be used after soaking. If you don't want to soak them, you can blend dried prunes into the drink of your choice – without soaking, dried prunes add a sweet, chewy, caramel consistency to your drinks. One thing we try to avoid is prune juice. It's usually made from concentrated juice, so has a lot of the nutritional value boiled out of it.

Goodnight Vienna

We say drink yourself healthy. You don't have to feel terrible in the morning, as long as you have lots of nice, fresh fruit with your alcohol. And this recipe is about as fruity as your greengrocer the time he wore that Carmen Miranda hat.

ingredients

5 guavas
2 large juicy peaches
100ml vodka
5 raspberries
Lots of ice

what to do

Cut the guavas in half and scoop out the flesh into the cocktail shaker.
Halve the peaches and remove the stone.
For once, put the peaches through the juicer, as you don't need the flesh.
Pour the peach juice into the cocktail shaker.
Add the vodka, raspberries and some ice to the shaker.
Shake hard and strain into two tall glasses filled with ice.

The science behind fruit and veg

Everyone knows that fruit and veg are very good for you. The NHS advise that the second most important thing you can do to reduce risk of cancer and heart disease is to eat more fruit and veg (the first is not to smoke), and the government has just embarked on a project to ensure that by 2004 every child gets a free piece of fruit each day at school. All good stuff as far as we're concerned.

Interestingly, while it is a proven scientific fact that eating fruit and veg reduces incidences of all major diseases, it is not yet fully understood why. Working with our friend and adviser Professor Joe Millward, we have attempted to explain the story so far. What you read below is Joe's explanation of how the nutrients in fruit and veg are essential to a healthy and happy life, minus a few of the big words.

Basically, it is essential to eat fruit and veg as they provide two main things:

Phytoprotectants
Essential non-antioxidant vitamins and minerals

Phytoprotectants
Phytoprotectants (phyto=plant) are the most important thing you can get out of juice. The term phytoprotectant is an umbrella that covers a complex group of

Antioxidants
Metabolic regulators
Hormone modifiers

Together, these guard against a whole range of ailments and disease, such as cancer, heart disease and strokes. Let's first look at antioxdants in more detail.

Antioxidants

Antioxidants are the good guys. They protect the body against the damaging effects of oxidisation (the same process that turns an apple brown once you've bitten into it). The best-known antioxidants are nutrients such as vitamins A, C, E, selenium and carotenoids (e.g. beta-carotene). None of these nutrients can be produced by the body, so we need to get supplies from elsewhere, with fruit and veg being the best source around.

The baddies responsible for the damaging process of oxidisation are unstable oxygen molecules known as free radicals. Free radicals are unstable as they only contain a single electron, so are always hungry to find a partner. In their quest to do this, they attack and damage healthy cells and transform DNA – the process that can lead to the development of cancers. Furthermore, free radicals can damage the fatty acids in your blood and induce the hardening of your arteries (atherosclerosis), which won't help your heart one bit.

Free radicals are a fact of life and are present in your body under normal circumstances from two main sources:

- Immune cells make free radicals to fight infections (to kill bacteria), so that maintaining the supply of antioxidants is especially important during infections, when free radicals will be in excess.

- All of the oxygen molecules we breathe in are converted to unstable free radicals during respiration.

Because of this natural presence, a diet rich in fruit and veg is necessary to ensure that the body receives the tools (the antioxidants) it needs to keep the free radicals in check.

However, additional free radicals can also come from the environment in which we live. A combination of pollution, fatty foods, cigarette smoke, alcohol and burnt toast is thought to contribute to their creation. So if you live in a city, smoke, drink and like burgers on toast, then you need to eat even more fruit and veg than your clean-living country counterparts.

Metabolic regulators

Metabolic regulators are another part of the phytoprotectants team. These substances, such as flavonoids and the coloured pigments present in many fruits and vegetables, control the 'fire' that burns during the constant process of metabolic change. Unchecked, the energy from this 'fire' can lead to changes in DNA that initiate cancer.

Cherries are a great example of a fruit that provides metabolic regulators, being blessed with the flavonoid queritrin, one of the most potent anti-cancer agents ever discovered. They are also rich in anthocyanins, the pigments that give them their rich red hue, and which are also being researched for their anti-cancer potential. Scientists continue to look into these areas as part of ongoing research into cancer prevention.

Hormone modifiers

It is thought that some cancers are caused by an imbalance of hormones in the body. For example, it's thought that an excess of hormones such as testosterone can stimulate prostate cancer cells. The same goes for breast cancer, where high levels of oestrogen in the body have been connected with an increased likelihood of breast and ovarian cancer.

Much research is being done into how the body controls and uses such hormones to avoid such imbalances. And although this area is not yet fully understood, fruit and veg is once again seen as being the source for the tools necessary for the body to go about its work.

Essential non-antioxidant vitamins and minerals

So fruit and veg supply phytoprotectants that have myriad benefits for your body. But in addition to phytoprotectants, fruit and veg provide key non-antioxidant vitamins and minerals, such as folate and potassium. These essential nutrients fulfill specific roles:

Folate – Helps the body form red blood cells, and is essential in the formation of healthy genetic material within the body's cells. Folate is considered especially important for young and pregnant women, and also works to prevent heart disease.

Potassium – Keeps your muscles and nerves healthy, and helps to keep the rhythm of your beating heart nice and regular. As a result of these attributes, it's a great all-round energy provider, which is why so many athletes are seen munching bananas, a fruit rich in potassium.

For more information, check the glossary.

The bottom line
…is that oranges don't just supply vitamin C, and bananas aren't only a good source of potassium. Fruit and veg provide an amazingly complicated combination of essential nutrients that work together in so many different ways to do us good. Scientists continue to research exactly how all of these components act together to make us healthy, and while it is far from fully understood, it is universally agreed that the key to good health lies in a varied and regular intake of fruit and veg, rather than relying on vitamin pills and supplements.

Vitamin pills simplify things too much by extracting certain segments of the nutritional parcel, without considering how the nutrients derived from fruit and veg work in harmony. Listening to a person play their part of a symphony on the triangle is not the same as hearing the whole orchestra play the same piece, just as munching vitamin pills can't come close to having a healthy and balanced diet.

So if you want to do one thing to give you a healthier and happier life, then make sure you're getting your five portions of fruit and veg a day. Your health will definitely improve for the better. The good news is that you don't need to move to a nunnery or give up the odd fry-up, you simply need to balance the bad things we all do with a few bits of goodness that your body will thank you for in years to come.

The glossary behind the science

Anti-carcinogens

Carcinogens are substances that cause cancer, and sources range from asbestos to bracken to tobacco smoke, but are mostly chemicals and chemical compounds that you've probably never heard of. Other sources include charred meat, brown bread crusts and basil, all high in various types of carcinogens. Luckily, many of the nutrients derived from fruit and veg, particularly vitamins C, E and beta-carotene, act as anti-carcinogens in limiting the effect of these cancer causing agents.

Antioxidants

Antioxidants are a huge group of nutrients that naturally occur in fruit and veg. They include vitamins C and E, and also beta-carotene, which the body can transform into vitamin A, and which has many great health properties of its own. Antioxidants keep your cells healthier longer. They prevent and repair the damage that can be done by free radicals.

Beta-carotene

This carotenoid is converted into vitamin A by the body. But beta-carotene is also an antioxidant in its own right, which protects against cancer and heart disease. You can usually tell fruit and veg which provide beta-carotene: – they will have pink or orange flesh, e.g. carrot, paw paw, pink grapefruit, nectarine.

Calcium

Everyone knows that calcium makes your teeth and bones nice and strong, so it's important to encourage children to take in their share of this wonder mineral. Calcium is also vital in the process of blood clotting, and is provided by dairy produce such as milk and yoghurt.

Carotenoids

The pigments that lend some fruits and veg their red, orange and yellow colouring. Acting as antioxidants, carotenoids strengthen the immune system and may lower the risk of heart disease, prevent some cancers, and protect against cataracts and macular degeneration, a disease that causes loss of sight in the central field of vision.

Of the many carotenoids found in fruit and veg, only six are thought to contribute greatly to our health – alpha-carotene, zeaxanthin, lycopene, lutein, cryptoxanthin and beta-carotene. Certain carotenoids, including alpha-carotene, cryptoxanthin and beta-carotene, are converted by the body into vitamin A, but only when required.

Flavonoids

Like carotenoids, flavonoids are plant pigments. They are found just under the skin of citrus fruit, amongst other places, and enable vitamin C to work properly and be absorbed into your cells. A study carried out by the US government in 2000 concluded that the 22 flavonoids found naturally in orange and tangerine juice seem to inhibit the growth of human cancer cells. Flavonoids are found in over 4,000 different types of fruit and veg, so you should be getting your dose if you are eating just about anything from your greengrocer's.

Folate/Folic acid

Folates are a group of folic-acid-related compounds essential for all; especially young women and pregnant women. Regular intake will prevent birth defects, lessen the risk of heart disease in middle aged men, and work against neurodegenerative disease (dementia) in the elderly. You can get your supply from citrus fruit, spinach and dried fruits.

Free radicals

Free radicals are unstable oxygen molecules that punch holes into our body's cellular walls, damaging DNA. Free radicals are unstable as they contain a single electron – without a partner, they cause imbalance in the body's chemical reactions. Pollution, tobacco smoke and a poor diet can lead to a proliferation of free radicals in the body. Antioxidants are the solution (see previous page).

Phytoprotectants

An umbrella term for the large family of nutrients supplied by fruit and veg.

Potassium

If you weigh about 70kg, there may be as much as 150g of potassium inside your body. Makes you think, doesn't it? Potassium activates the particular enzymes that give you energy (that's why athletes are always eating bananas), and also ensures properly functioning cells, leading to healthy muscles, nerves and heart. Get your potassium from a wide range of fresh fruit and veg.

Selenium

Another nutrient classed as an antioxidant, selenium is a powerful soldier in the fight against free radicals. Selenium also helps out when it comes to preventing heart disease and prostate cancer, and it promotes healthy eyes, hair and skin. Some studies have shown that those who live in areas of low selenium soils have more cancer and heart complaints than those living in areas of high selenium soils. In case you're interested, Norfolk has the most selenium-rich soil in the UK, while the rest of Europe and the USA are pretty low.

Vitamin A

As with all vitamins, this is a substance that our bodies cannot naturally produce. Therefore, we need to obtain it from an outside source. Vitamin A is essential for all-round good health, particularly vision and growth. It also maintains healthy skin cells, slowing the outward effects of ageing, and bolsters the immune system. Vitamin A doesn't directly occur in veg, but beta-carotene (a precursor of vitamin A) does.

Vitamin C

The best known of all vitamins, vitamin C is vital for healthy bones, teeth and blood. It will also protect against cancers, heart disease and bolster the immune system. It's prevalent in all citrus fruits, while kiwi is also a good provider.

Vitamin E

This vitamin protects the heart and maintains healthy blood vessels. As with vitamins A and C, it shores up the immune system and also acts as an anti-blood-clotting agent.

Organic produce – some innocent thoughts

Over the last few years, the issue of organic foods has received a huge amount of media attention and consumer interest. Organic produce once had the image of being strictly for hippies, Earth mothers and your R.E. teacher, but has increasingly found more space both on shop shelves and in the national press.

The debate over whether or not organic produce is better for you continues at the time of writing this little book. Our stance is simple; if the concept of eating organically means you are more predisposed to eating fruit and veg, then it is a good thing. Anything that encourages people to eat more of that life-enhancing, diet-friendly, friends-impressing stuff we call fruit and veg has to be welcomed with open arms. But whatever you do, don't let an absence of organic produce stop you from eating fruit and veg. And don't fall into the trap of thinking that by buying a box of organic doughnuts and a bottle of organic gin you are being healthy. Natural fruit and veg are the key to a healthy diet – organic or otherwise.

Our little drinks are obviously completely natural, but at the time of writing they are not organic. This is for several reasons, the main one being that the case for organics has not been proved from a nutritional point of view. At the time of writing, the Food Standards Agency has ruled that there is no substantiation of Soil Association claims that organic is better for you. And while not many people realise this, certain chemicals can be used in organic farming, and tend to be used in high doses as they are not that effective. In our opinion, it is the industrialisation of farming that is the bigger problem – not necessarily whether the food has been grown organically or not. Organic agriculture used to be synonymous with non-intensive farming but this is now not always the case.

A second issue for us is that going organic does limit choice, and we need to get the right variety of fruit, from the right plantations, at the right time of year, to consistently produce drinks that make you go 'yum'. Finally, making our drinks organically would, at present, increase the price so that it would be out of reach to most consumers. Our drinks are already on the pricey side, simply because we use fruit and nothing else, so we're nervous about putting the price up and going organic.

Ultimately, we strive to do what is best for the fruit and best for the drinker, not what the media is promoting as this week's story. And while debates such as organic versus non-organic continue, there is one fact that every knowledgeable person agrees on: that the most effective thing you can do to improve your diet is to eat a load more fruit and veg in any form – organic, fresh, frozen, even canned. It's all good stuff, and we should all be eating as much of it as possible.

Shopping for ready-made juice

Very often, you'll buy juice in the supermarket for your fridge at home, or from the sandwich shop for your lunch. So how do you make an informed decision? We hope to enlighten you with this guide, and point out the goodies and baddies of the juice world.

Remember, when it comes to fruit juice labels, everything may not be as it first appears. If you want to find out what is actually in your drink, study the ingredients panel very carefully.

The following explanations should make things a lot clearer:

Concentrates
A lot of bottled fruit juices are 'from concentrate'. Concentrates are made by taking a fruit juice, heating it to a high temperature and evaporating off the water. This leaves a thick syrup that is a small proportion of the original volume (as low as 12% with oranges). This is packed in drums, frozen and shipped across the world. At the bottling stage, the syrup is defrosted and water is added back to blend the juice up to its normal strength. Some manufacturers then use things called 'add backs' to give the juice a 'fresh' aroma and compensate for the effect of concentrating.

The sole reason for concentrating a juice is to reduce shipping and storage costs. It is definitely not in the best interests of the fruit or the person drinking it. You will never find concentrated juices in our smoothies.

Crush
A crush is a drink made from fruit juice, purées, water and sugar. As it's watered down, it is thinner than a 100% fruit juice or smoothie, but can be quite refreshing.

Freshly squeezed
Fresh is the magic word. This means that the juice has come from fruit that has been brought into the UK, squeezed locally and put into a bottle. This means that the fruit juice has not been tampered with – and it's certainly not concentrated. Therefore, it will taste great and have the best possible nutritional profile.

Juice drink

A juice drink is not a fruit juice. It can contain as little as 5% fruit juice, with the rest being water/sugar/even vegetable oil – basically, anything to bulk it out and make it cheaper.

Not from concentrate (NFC)

If a product is not from concentrate (NFC), then it has been made with juice that hasn't been concentrated. The juice isn't freshly squeezed but it hasn't been reduced to a syrup. Typically an NFC product is made by importing frozen blocks of juice into the UK, defrosting the juice, sometimes adding back some natural juice flavouring and then bottling it. NFC juice is not as good as freshly squeezed, but it's much better than juice from concentrate.

Pasteurisation

There are two types of pasteurisation: gentle and UHT.

Gentle or flash pasteurisation is the process that happens to all of the fresh milk that you buy and to some juices. It involves heating the juice quickly for a brief period of time to a moderate temperature. It does not affect the product: all nutritional properties remain the same and (if done well) it's impossible to taste the difference. Fresh juice is pasteurised to knock out bugs – when you're making smoothies at scale and putting in the whole fruit, you don't want to take any risks. A US smoothie company didn't pasteurise its juice and unfortunately this resulted in outbreak of e-coli which killed one person and hospitalised many others. In the US, if you don't pasteurise your fresh juice, you have to put a health warning on the label.

UHT pasteurisation is the same process that produces long-life milk. This involves heating the drink to a very high temperature, which kills all bugs present. This does affect the product – long-life milk doesn't taste that great and a UHT pasteurised fruit juice just doesn't have the same nutritional quality as other juice. It is used to remove anything from the juice that would cause it to go off, so the product can sit on a shelf for months without anything happening, which is not what nature intended.

Pure/100% fruit

If a product is pure juice or 100% fruit, then there is nothing in the product apart from juice. However, the product may not be fresh and it could be made from concentrate. It is always worth checking the ingredients panel, because if a juice is from concentrate, it should be declared.

Pure squeezed

This is the same as 'not from concentrate'. It does not mean fresh – the fruit will have been squeezed in another country, frozen and shipped to the UK.

Smoothie

A real smoothie is a blend of crushed and freshly squeezed fruit. It should be 100% pure fruit with no added sugar or water and, most importantly, be made with fresh rather than concentrated juices. A smoothie will be thicker and more pulpy than a normal juice as it contains whole crushed fruit.

Thickie

A stupid name we made up for our yoghurt drinks. We call them this because they are like our smoothies, but a bit thicker.

Index

Index

My recipe

ingredients

what to do

My recipe

ingredients

what to do

My recipe

ingredients

what to do

My recipe

ingredients

what to do

If you've filled up all of these pages, you really should come and work at Fruit Towers.

173

Notes

Notes

Getting in touch

Having trouble peeling your mangoes? Then pop round to see us at Fruit Towers:

innocent drinks
Fruit Towers
3 Goldhawk Estate
Brackenbury Road
London W6 0BA

Or ring the banana phone on 020 8600 3939, or even email toughmangoes@innocentdrinks.co.uk
And if you're bored why not visit www.innocentdrinks.co.uk?

From left to right:
Richard Reed, Dan Germain, Lucy Ede and Adam Whitaker.